sensorium

AKRON SERIES IN POETRY

AKRON SERIES IN POETRY
Mary Biddinger, Editor

Emily Corwin, *Sensorium*
Kimberly Quiogue Andrews, *A Brief History of Fruit*
Joshua Harmon, *The Soft Path*
Oliver de la Paz, *The Boy in the Labyrinth*
Krystal Languell, *Quite Apart*
Brittany Cavallaro, *Unhistorical*
Tyler Mills, *Hawk Parable*
Caryl Pagel, *Twice Told*
Emily Rosko, *Weather Inventions*
Emilia Phillips, *Empty Clip*
Anne Barngrover, *Brazen Creature*
Matthew Guenette, *Vasectomania*
Sandra Simonds, *Further Problems with Pleasure*
Leslie Harrison, *The Book of Endings*
Emilia Phillips, *Groundspeed*
Philip Metres, *Pictures at an Exhibition: A Petersburg Album*
Jennifer Moore, *The Veronica Maneuver*
Brittany Cavallaro, *Girl-King*
Oliver de la Paz, *Post Subject: A Fable*
John Repp, *Fat Jersey Blues*
Emilia Phillips, *Signaletics*
Seth Abramson, *Thievery*
Steve Kistulentz, *Little Black Daydream*
Jason Bredle, *Carnival*
Emily Rosko, *Prop Rockery*
Alison Pelegrin, *Hurricane Party*
Matthew Guenette, *American Busboy*
Joshua Harmon, *Le Spleen de Poughkeepsie*

Titles published since 2011.
For a complete listing of titles published in the series,
go to www.uakron.edu/uapress/poetry.

sensorium

EMILY CORWIN

The University of Akron Press
Akron, Ohio

ISBN: 978-1-629221-54-0 (paper)
ISBN: 978-1-629221-67-0 (ePDF)
ISBN: 978-1-629221-68-7 (ePub)

LIBRARY OF CONGRESS CATALOGING-IN-PUBLICATION DATA
Names: Corwin, Emily (Poet), author.
Title: Sensorium / Emily Corwin.
Description: First edition. | Akron, Ohio : The University of Akron Press, 2020. | Series: Akron
  series in poetry
Identifiers: LCCN 2019046211 (print) | LCCN 2019046212 (ebook) | ISBN 9781629221540
  (paperback ; alk. paper) | ISBN 9781629221670 (pdf) | ISBN 9781629221687 (epub)
Subjects: LCGFT: Poetry.
Classification: LCC PS3603.O7924 S46 2020 (print) | LCC PS3603.O7924 (ebook) |
  DDC 811/.6--dc23
LC record available at https://lccn.loc.gov/2019046211
LC ebook record available at https://lccn.loc.gov/2019046212

∞The paper used in this publication meets the minimum requirements of ANSI/NISO z39.48–
1992 (Permanence of Paper).

Cover image: iStock photo by Jekaterina Voronina. Cover design by Amy Freels.

Sensorium was designed and typeset in Garamond by Amy Freels and printed on sixty-pound
natural and bound by Bookmasters of Ashland, Ohio.

Affordable
Learning Initiative
THE UNIVERSITY OF AKRON

Produced in conjunction with the University
of Akron Affordable Learning Initiative.
More information is available at
www.uakron.edu/affordablelearning/

For Joe and Soup

Contents

sensorium

1

in dappled sun, in wine sap apples
I dab prismatic gloss atop my cupid's

    bow—the philtrum it's called, it's
    chrome-like. I have a mouth & it stinks—

this is where I masticate the animal
brisket, the pie pumpkin & red plums,

    pomegranate tannins. I dream inside
    a jewelcasket, misted in microcrystalline.

2

inside the sensorium, the body of me
is delightful, delighted to meet you. you become

all atremble, my apple powder, my allergy. fit yourself
between my two palms, longing with bile & black-eyed susans.

    I will make us a drink mostly ice chips, Chambourcin in a stemless glass.
    I will bring us an onset of fever.

3

this bed of dead roses & tuberose & rosehips & hawthorns, this drool
& booger. this floater in the eye—shred-like, collagen fleck. a squiggle,

    a garter snake in my garden patch. I shudder as it goes by, in direct sun. I wish
    I could extract it, show you my protein. in the sensorium, in drearsome nest

of yellow jacket bumble—my dear, my moon pie—I spy something red & boiled
& glazen. a wax fruit, fruit wax to slide over my stink. won't you come hither,

      come whether or not you like my leather miniskirt, my ether anesthetic—
      help me onto the gurney, I won't flinch.

4

hurtle down the hallway, hurtle down the hedgerows. I flush & ooze,
my mucus membrane something horrible. scab-picker, I make it worse

      —slough off the carapace, the gelled cream & jello shots.
      I'm afraid this is how things get when I forget my dosage—

fluoxetine to keep the creepy crawlies at bay. my ribs—breakable
rungs to be wrung then rolled out into fondant for the spongecake.

5

my sensorium, my prism—plum-red, atremble.
I feel the onset of fever now. now, I come home

      to the medical bed, cold-blooded & spectral—this,
      my casket of jewels. this, my crystal & microbes.

my body glitter, it strobes, chrome-like. dunk me into
the wine jug. pin me up for apple bobbing, embossed

      like a rosebud—so gorgeous, so gorged with feeling.

Outburst as Carrie White

After *Carrie* (1976)

Help me into the pail of redblack pig—
hemoglobin and craft glitter plastered to

    my every hair tendril, sausage curls. I am
    dunked in bridesilk, tinsel blush, soft focus

        nipple—my boudoir mirror puckers at me.
        The rotten girls won't shut up ever, they snicker

    under bleachers, streamers, electrocution dust.
    Help me to the infirmary, please, into the doctor's

bag, to Momma's catholic shawl. Why did no one
tell me about the bloodslit, about gymnasium kiss,

    carnations stick-pinned over aortas? I am so over you,
    Momma, no apple tea for me. All these pigs over the

        resin fence picket—I have a ruby-red hammer;
        I know how to use it.

traumata

in a hemorrhage from the eye | in a modem, my cranium blotted like a morgue and I am repulsed | my amygdala seems to hate me | it jolts when I see him, near-dead | across my high-gloss plastic screen | I crumple under an eiderdown duvet | I purr enormously, sordid on the deathbed | he never looks away, not elsewhere | he beholds me and I behold a horror, an eyesore | I imbibe a Venus in Furs, in a flute glass dashed with orange zest and bitters | the mortuary won't take me | I so long to be mindless, heartless, no longer gnarled by pictures, ghastly and incessant | entomb me | put my little viscera in the ground, with Prozac and an android phone | synthetic glow, the lambent halogen | the mortuary won't take me like this | not with my eye-bleed | my couture dress blotted with oranges | sore and sordid, hateful amygdala | my cranium jiggles and I behold a tomb | my bloomers unbloomed | near-dead, I purr like a modem tired from usage | the modified release dosage from the orange pill bottle | it keeps him apart from me | the boy with hemorrhage, his viscera incessant, aglow | I so long to be heartless, mindless | a happy blank | in the mortician's nimble fingertips | I turn back, returning to bacterium | a slipper animalcule | glob in a pipette

splint

oh you, you must live to be hush, my honeydew
—I have to have you, your ankle, your hormone,
the ladybirds twisting there against your scalp.

I never want to check my email ever again today.
never want the copious blood in my hole. I would hate
to be left on the cool, white stairs without any rosebuds

from the bachelor. and today, in the strawberries,
in the sepals, a dead baby sugar-ant. such tiny beings
tend to sicken me. how many have fed me, on accident?

haven't they carried me all this while? and recently, truthfully,
I couldn't find any pictures of kindness. I will party all night
if I have to, I will show my face all day if I have to. I am still so

pink at the center—cold-armed and mortal with my socket click,
my chipped julep nails, fluorescent as status updates. I dread
any length of time alone with myself, ashen like a wax museum.

I long to wilt into your breast pocket and be carried home.
oh my hush, I thought myself unlovable for so long. maybe I was
made for this soft tissue, this taut buckle of yours. oh, to go with
you into the coffins, to see lilac in that darkest staircase.

Outburst as Laurie Strode

After *Halloween* (1978)

In Haddonfield, Illinois, I wait in a fiberglass
desk, on the rotary phone. I am *Laurie dear.* I don't wanna

> hear about Bob, Paul, or Ben. No sheet ghost, no harlequin
> clown with a hacksaw. Every town has something like this—

>> heartleaf philodendron on the back patio and cheese pumpkin,
>> porcelain doll pumpkin, sugar dumpling squash, golden nugget.

> The pendulum clock tolls—I moan like a flying saucer, stagger
> along the foyer in a torn pinafore. The hospital smocks wither,

oh somebody please, oh god I did not mean to scare you
away. Cut with me into the hairgrass, the fibrous strands—

> a shape guttering behind the clothespins. Oh god,
> somebody please—there are gowns blustering out in the

>> prairie, white patient gowns congested with Thorazine.

Outburst as Rosemary Woodhouse

After Rosemary's Baby (1968)

I can no longer abide the tonic,
the coltsfoot, mugwort, and burdock—

    a mild sedative that Dr. Saperstein prescribes.
    I am put under, put below—a tourniquet on

        the tricep, a mouse bite, convulsions in a
        rabid tapping beneath my maternity frock

    and stiff Peter Pan collar and the cranberry stockings
    gotten loose. Come on out Little Andy or Jenny,

I have defrosted the sirloin for you, no longer
devil's pepper glutting the umbilical cord. I won't

    begone from you, never into morphine drip or coma.
    They gave you a pram—sable-black brocade. Little Andy

        or Jenny, I am not okay. Can we start all over? My angel
        -food and margarine, my precious hellion. How could I not

recognize you? Having dragged you with me
all this while, intimate as a blood sample.

nuptial

After "Bluebeard"

how came this clot and
platelet. how came my palms
releasing a door ajar—old
murder there, soured body
there, and another and another
and mother, how could you let
me come to this? how came
myself to see the sacrum, tibia
stripped like that? how came
the shudder under me like a
tall light guttering across the
corridor. how came this man
who says: *don't go there, don't
you dare.* I dared, mother,
I didn't believe the vicious
pulsing in him. and now,
how many things can become
protection, become weapon—a
ladle, colander, needle eye,
letter opener. mother, you
always said I was sharp and I
am, in his bedroom, seeking to
pierce, to make incision.

traumata

I feel crummy—   crumbling against a Plexiglas door—

    never horses—   fitful at my door—   never to take me off—

    to the morgue—   just flocks of barn swallow breast—

phlox between my shellac manicure—   no hangnail—   just
    hobnail—

for the pinebox I faint into—   too much Sudafed—   no antihistamines
    could save me—

    from that hemorrhage—   his tremor I tremble at—   jolted with
    winter static—

    my synthetic plasticine dress—   shocks even myself—   would I be
    considered—

a basket case—   could you lay me—   in a basket—   a wicker picnic
     hamper—

like an ejected foal—   I didn't make it long—

     in this world, oxygenated—   rusted through with plasma—

crepuscule

maybe I am just meant to be awful.
awfully quiet, I am meant to crumple
in a tulip dress, ruched bodycon, my
gauzy bralette peeking at the sternum.

I keen against you and you're such a beaut,
my man-candy, my love-person. we slide
beside the evening natatorium, pool chlorine
makes of me a prune. but who cares really, in

the scheme of things, the scene of us blithesome
in the duskiness, gloom-struck. I ruck up my
silhouette, its gothic skirting. you reach beneath,
switch me on and the hormone starts to drip.

Outburst as Clarice Starling

After The Silence of the Lambs (1991)

What became of my lamb fleece in the still dark,
      in its tufted fur pupa? Flushingly, I sigh inside my

           peacoat with the toggle buttons, Virginia fog, stud
    sterling earring, skin cream and the camphor ointment

under the nose when viewing a body, the missing girl's
      collegiate blouse—post-mortem against the slab. In her,

           there was stellate entrance wound between thoracic
    vertebrae, ligature mark, soft palate blurred grayish in

gunpowder damp from Elk River. The doctors told me: *Don't
    get near to the glass.* They fed me intravenously—the nightshade,

           clover honey lump. I say *good evening* and the cocoon loosens.
    There is a man I seek—he will hiss at me and it is just a scratch.

Outburst as Heather Donahue

After The Blair Witch Project (1999)

Gone off the face of this earth, I appear a little blurry, a vapor—
my feet never touch the ground, not ragweed, foxtail, beardtongue.

Fuck, it's cold. Upon the leaves, I brush my fur. Hello? Hello you? I'm
sorry to everyone I know. I think we should get our fingers gaping, the

bloodstream—there's no baby scream, is there? Maybe it could be the
deer, bleating between the scarlet oaks? All around us, the sound of film

burns, light leak, steps. We're out of cigarettes. Do I look like I'm laughing?
This is America, this is Burkittsville, Tappy Creek, Coffin Rock, this is a house

moldering asbestos. It can't be true, it can't be you under the plaster,
under plastic—brought out of the woods in a white, spectral pouch.

Outburst as Thomasin

After *The VVitch* (2015)

Let's to the wood and I will vanish you   your spirit smeared
     under my riding cloak, my waistcoat   smock and petticoat
     sugarloaf hat

     kerchief   let me scrub your woolens and billhook   I will keep secret
about the wood   *clickety clackety*   there you are   I will have you for
    meat cutlet

there you are   your fibula wriggles   on the chopping block
     the leg-hold trap   beseech me not   I slurp, wagging my jaws in a
     yolk sac

the chick never incubated   never eggtooth   a baby in a butter churn
     baa baa baa   Black Philip holds fast   he gallops against my lumbar disc

     myself undressed   I confess: I have been delicious as satin tinseled
I'll be in field, rid of my kindred reek   stockings off   what went we out
    to find

     if not wolves, athirst   I dangle from the jack pines
     sucking on a silver chalice.

scab-picker

remove pores clogged in oil across nose
tip and septum, remove chin whisker,
upper lip hairs and white hairs and pit
hairs and pubic hairs and tit hairs,
remove eyelash no time to wish, remove
mucus secretion from glands and rheum
discharge, remove tampon within eight
hours of insertion, remove gastric acid
and deciduous tooth, remove dirt clod
from navel and throat sludge, plantar
wart, crusted scab, too-long nail, sparkle,
synthetic wax smudge under eye and
spittle, remove skin altogether, make spic
and span, until the end, the undermost,
stripped all to the pith.

wound care

the ankle blister from pleather shoe strap & buckle—I
insisted to be dressed in pumps & a fuzzy black velour
babydoll, & then there is razor burn over my tibia,
headaching from rum with raspberry shrub, tonic water,
dry vermouth. unwrapped my everything & I am riven—a
black tampon sizzling out, vaginal clot like beef liver. I am
one big itch & I hate it. wouldn't it be nice to stay up all
hours & gossip with myself about so-and-so & how I
thought I saw him behind me on I-75 & he stayed there
trailing my ass, even when I went over the rumble strips &
if that's not love. I do not want to trash the lamb's ear, but
this caught bouquet, it smells & I don't know how much
good it is going to do for me.

Outburst as Nina Sayers

After *Black Swan* (2010)

the cuticle peeled back and metatarsal | I thrust back into my toe
box | stretch taut the drawstring | footed tights with gusset | resin
is crushed against the slipper | it shudders | I am nothing at all |
but a pancake tutu in grapefruit blush| camisole leotard and pale
houndstooth holding a laced drink | a rash under a coat of black
feather quills | I am nothing at all ever | but a glissade in a birdcage
veil | I snarl | my diaphragm contracting | I fouetté beneath a
coronet of burnt copper | encrusted bodice| how is my skin? |
have I left it alone awhile? | it is nothing | to me | white grease
around the under-eyes | and I am not your Nina | I am not Nina at
all | I grind myself down to a hairpin | my headpiece goes brittle |
it decomposes| upon a mangled looking glass

traumata

undo my oxblood gown in a briar patch,
gushing. undo the video—the polar bear
starved, atrophied. undo eye-bleed.
undo flute glass and Prozac dose. undo
my father bent in sickness, undo the
exam table paper. undo ulcer of mine,
undo gastritis—acid like hooklets. undo
the wood creak, the creek and woods.
undo nerve-ending and protozoa. undo
bauble, gimcrack, scrimshaw brimming
on my bedside table. undo delirium.
undo my last comment. undo my
disorder, I am out of order and need
maintenance. undo the video, videos
of men bent in death throes. undo fish
oil pills, undo my own heart repulsive.
place it inside enamel dresser box,
replace the frail tendon, my chest
incandescent with starbright

Outburst as Marion Crane

After *Psycho* (1960)

Offer me a tranquilizer and I won't say no—
this headache, achingly real as Wonder Bread.

    Waist-slip, bullet bra, cluck of the sling-back
    kitten heels, and I won't spend the weekend

        in bed—I have my hard-shell valise and speedometer.
        I'd really rather not, not stop someplace, not go

    into the fruit cellar, to the body cavities of barn owls,
    taken to with the forceps. I crinkle like a motel soap,

stripped of its wrapper, waxen. Please, do not think me
uncaring—I am in a great hurry, am hurried off to someplace

    impeccable, cuspid-sharp, bloodless as an envelope.

Outburst as Mary Henry

After *Carnival of Souls* (1962)

And then the lake went down. And then they made a dancehall of it.
My combed-back bouffant, my wiggle dress bunched—does the hem

hang right in the back? I never heard such goings-on. Why, I never.
Doctor, you've got to tell me what to do. I am off my rocker, off and over

the truss bridge, to the water with all the mud it's carrying. How is it a window
becomes my mirror at night? Two panes of glass, two smears blinking back—

dissatisfied, so quiet-like. This used to be quite the place. You could hide
a man in every corner. Doctor, I guess you took it wrong last night. It wouldn't

be seemly to you, to skitter beneath crepe paper streamers, the devil roiling
with his blood hounds. I am cast out, no more tabernacle. Thank you, but
I am never coming back.

zoloft diary

today, I am my best self: sedated,
watered, made neat as pins and needlework.

a squirming happens, the stomach—
rabid mammal, slack jawed with acid.

dear void, dear whoever:
today, I took it one day at a time

a small blue seed streaking my insides.

pain management

my balconette bra pinches—I flinch
under the underwire like an unhappy
trout. there is nowhere to be loud and
the crescent moon kept its eye on me,
kept buying me gin & tonics with a
sharp lime wedge, immaculately square
ice. I crouch on the laminate, keeping
still on my hind legs, hind wings. I keep
silence below each dress layer. you ask if
I am *like, ordinary emotional or, like,
really emotional?* I dust a shadow called
cobbler on my crease & lid. I know you
will like it—just click there on the heart.

poem comprised of lipstick shades

in the afterdark, in your slowburn acid wash,
I strip my catsuit at the zipper like a sext, like

    a spank from the moshpit, like a wrong number
    call from a bianca. you made me like this—jilted,

        ex-girlfriend bumbling through the grape jelly, rum
        donuts, popsicles, and bang rabbits. you said I can

    be a brat and I hate it—I curtsy for you in a tulle
    and jacquard screenshot, your stepford cheerleader,

        an amulet of tipsy daiquiris, old roses.

Outburst as Ivy Walker

After The Village (2004)

What manner of spectacle—
what out of Covington Woods?

    The livestock taken, ravaged complete—
    such quarts of blood, much of the fur

consumed, it seems. What culprit?
What creature or vertebrate clacking

    there, in robes burst red as chokecherries,
    raked up, then buried down, down ever.

We must keep careful watch across
the Resting Rock, the hills and thunderclap.

    I am but scared. I must leave to the towns,
    to retrieve medicines, return with haste.

I must away with my drawstring sack,
my cape of mustard seed, blotched,

    crudely in muck. The buckthorn that
    grows—I'm going where I ought not go.

sickroom

this mess of dress—gown blown back, a bundle

    of buttermilk. inside her trundle-bed, the beading

        and the sewing thread, throwing limbs, throes and

    sighing. the nightstand standing by, with lye soaps

and rind of lime. we trim her chest with tourniquets,

    the minutes dim and quieting. she squints to see

        the trillium, mums and lawn she's missing, the mist

    as low as sin. the invalid, her rusted jaw,

        moving maw with crumb

Outburst as Ginger Fitzgerald

After Ginger Snaps (2000)

You big suck, you're really glooming. How smooth
it was made—that thing in the road, a disc of epidermis.

    Life in Bailey Downs—the branches break into cake flour.
    The girls are adolescent, they spill cornflowers, corn syrup,

their woolen skirts knife-pleated. I am to leave forever,
for a shallow-made grave. Just look at the worms,

    composting, the failed monkshood. I'll behave, I'll be
    good now, don't rat me out. I'm not off to some

rubber motel. I blow, I am blown out, the lycanthrope eye
of mine bucking and baying, a hound lapping up cherry.

Outburst as Nancy Thompson

After A Nightmare on Elm Street (1984)

Hey dickhead, hey creep—I'll punch your lights out,
no biggie, no freak out. Your arms widen like a harrow,

    spiked, slashing at my pin-tucked nightie, my boot-cut
    jeans you can't catch ever. I won't be dragged along,

sobbing like some Tina into body bags or garment bags
or hands of paramedics. Screw the coroner, screw the

    maggot and screeching in the bougainvillea, the rose trellis
    you stand on. My eyebrows don't have time for you. I turn

my bed down—it becomes a grave mound, a bump rising
up like bread yeast, blistering—a boiled sarcophagus.

aerial

After "Thumbelina"

I'm a poor little thing, I'm deep
    underground sewing a coverlet of

    mint leaves, sewing my trousseau
for bedding & wedding Mr. Mole,

my dreadful spindle, my lighted touchwood
    in the tunnels. and I can sit on your back,

    my nuthatch, despite that wing,
shred under the hawthorn. look at the sun,

    on all of us now. will you dissect the
        damselfly—give me what is mine?

residence in a time of horror

it was something gloomy out there—in the gloaming, in the ground
that gives, ground that takes. yes, it is a brutal planet we have, it says:

danger, do not enter. and what direction are you running, love? did it hurt to be
outside? under the local meadow, blood invades, the virus moaning delicious

into wilder life. what is there to do but tremble, become a softer element,
supple, foraging for antidote—a small, ardent berry to reside here, to resist.

villanelle w/ anxious thoughts

please do for me a kindness
I require you near, softly as software.
my brain misfire, this mental illness.

I trash the household knives—hideous,
coruscating into the waste basket, the serrated
glinting, too much. I saw them jabbed, unkind

and hazardous in my eye's puncta. my own impulses,
manic. I take to rosé cider and naps, ever so scared
of myself and others. please refuse me the machines. it is

my compulsion to search-engine, seek the incubus.
I type, I like to frighten me with diseases, I dare
to see cardiac event, asphyxiation, viscera outside its rind.

I despise the web, know of what it's capable—distress,
apprehension, long sobbing over a polycarbonate carapace.
don't you think I would make a happy animatronic, never ill

but operational, functional automaton, my skull—one of stillness?
the knives glare sullen in the can, under pink lady apples, price tags, hair
follicle. they scrape there, pleading me to do their bidding, the peeled eye. can
I abide this and how long? this gripping neurosis, this never-desired, this vicious.

traumata

repulsive as a loose hemorrhage—   I am a lambchop—

       under halogen lamps—   heart anatomized—

           parted—   he won't part from me—

never apart from the psychic apparatus—   boy with the dashed
   cranium—

     coins against the eyelids, sordid—   the boy entombed—

I long to—   clamber there beside him—

behold and hold his ghastly facial bone—   delete the capillary

snapped—

we belong in a mortuary—   my own cadaver in metallic lamé—

couture boots in charcoal black pleather—   together now, we

crumple—

                                        beneath a blotted screen—

Outburst as Melanie Daniels

After The Birds (1963)

All at once they bury me—the strawberry finches
flapping, how they perforate, pricking like booster

shots for tetanus. Cover your faces, cover your brandy
in the snifter glass. I think now, now, now it's the crows

again, oh I think so—it's just no good. A body molting.
A peck on the cheek is slippery. Try not to think at all.

My flaked manicure around the coiled phone cable.
My bouclé dress suit—honeydew green, aflutter under

a loud stripe of mandibles, a ringed eye breathing.

Outburst as Becky Driscoll

After *Invasion of the Body Snatchers* (1956)

There's our evening. I turn up like paraffin burning in your haystack,
in the south pasture. How I hate to drag you out of bed at this hour.

Botched with the pitchfork, prickling in my gingham strapless with the bolero.
Mine was not an ordinary body. Maybe the result of atomic radiation in the

surrounding plant and animal life. Too late to warn the others, inconsolable.
I become reanimated, become the host—I am making spoon bread. No, no, you

mustn't go near it. In the hothouse, in gestation, I am slaked in sodium,
carbonated. A face pasted on, the dimensions almost that of a woman.
Almost yours.

bauble

maybe near Coldwater or Jackson or Cass River—a Shell station off I-69 N, it was where I extracted it, the ring from my left pointer finger when hand-washing in the restroom because it would keep damp, make discomfort, discomfit me—the chalcedony in a silver bezel. did not feel its lack, misplaced placement, not for another two hours. it was some ways south, mileages away, unknown. distraught, I was: agitated as from emotional conflict, as made asunder, to stretch, taut. I called myself distraught and an idiot. there was no time for compassion. I lack patience as well as jewelry. I had lasted 355 miles of unlit Midwest hotcake flat—made so by a glacier, the Laurentide ice sheet in the Quaternary period 2.6 million years from me weepily driving with dark nothings in the rear-view. I had lasted half a year of twisted foot and crutch, of cruel email, of puke, now of lost ring. no thing seems declarative to me in winters, not arresting, no thing to impress upon the eye—I scour the vanishing point ahead, sour with a certain luster.

ghazal with the city sparking

across my computer, my glass confession screen, a city
everyone should wish for. apparently, I am not *cut-out* for cities,

(according to him) so I crinkle along in a three-dollar ballroom
crinoline mess, in my best Midwest: *sorry, you're right, I'm sorry,* sitting

on a pile of coneflowers, asters, tart cherries & a newborn
deer baby. I guess I am just not cool enough for his city,

not a glamazon or powerhouse or a somebody. I guess this sugar
pie won't eat itself, I guess this house will do with electricity

enough & some antique copper & cabbage roses & honey goat cheese,
bramble vodka, Kroger handsoap, arugula. would this be called *simplicity*

—to not have a high-rise or scraped sky? for staying among
the verdant acreage & turnpikes never headed for cities.

oh, sweetened girl, don't stand there being wishful, wistful like
a drooped fist. city or no city, there is glinting still for seeing.

dark webs

a slow phone charge, a payment made successfully. you can
follow my lifetime anytime. you can click here for more. my
room collects a season: bucket bag, triple sec, fanny pack,
cat sticker, plate crumbs, slapped mosquito scum. low
battery always. convinced I am dying always. instead
of paying the electric, I buy a sheer romper, a pale
kinderwhore dress. question: why would anyone buy cheese
online? also: why is that something you can actually do?
across a flume of mist, I missed you, sweating like a spit-
roast suckling pig in a charmeuse nightslip, on a balcony,
waiting to unbuckle you.

sanctum

in my heart of hearts, in my darkish green & horizontal branches, I consume a granulated sugar—I need enough to waken. a measure of protection—I curl inward in a ringlet, careful now. & over the garden wall—the bitter gourd, the vegetable marrow unmoving, here & there, plant lobe & cellule & sediment, not withered, not yet. this is my living, flecked everywhere with various plastics: polymer, polyester, polyamide items that surround the surroundings. back to my lakebed & bedcovers. the insides, the outsides of me get stung, my morning body never a morning glory, more like: no thank you, more like today is not the best day for anything.

traumata

no thank you demon with the powder blue iris no thank you my sinuses
which crackle no thank you sludge no thank you thalamus and dopamine
synapse no thank you cardiovascular ward no thank you my father's eye and
capillary no thank you rib-eye I have not touched a meat since then no thank
you Google incessant no thank you I require SSRIs for my life no thank you
I can doze on my dosage for fifteen hours in a day no thank you I sleep as
freedom no thank you genetic makeup no thank you makeup applicator over
my chin the scab enduring for six good months no thank you cholesterol no
thank you blood pressure cuff no thank you I lock up my small machines out
of sight I am to the woods without network my vision taintless as Waterford
crystal as a slipper of silica glass

Outburst as Marcie Cunningham

After *Friday the 13th* (1980)

Braless, my midriff flaunted, I am a speck in a thicket of
racer-snakes, small forest axe in my temple, my temporal

lobe tacked to the wall. *Milk and honey on the other side
hallelujah.* The wind's come up. It makes me wanna hold

to you. We're totally doomed. A bunch of fires out here,
so they say, at Camp Crystal Lake, Camp Blood. That clatter

in the outhouse, how it hushes fast like valium. Oh come on
you guys, okey dokey now, olly olly oxen free! I yelp a little

in my undergarments, my face weeping under the weapon.

Outburst as Jay Height

After It Follows (2014)

What is the matter \ what is it \ it is a
person \ then it isn't \ I flee from it \ I
rush into Plymouth \ Sterling Heights \
Wolverine Lake \ have you seen it \ seen
me \ I'm so pretty \ it's annoying \
winged liquid eye \ Sherpa jacket \ cowrie
shells about the jugular \ who is it there \
what is it I'm running from \ chloroform
moistening my sinuses \ a really cute guy
\ it eats my Doritos and white bread
sandwich \ prowls naked on the roof
shingles \ what is it that twists my leg all
back \ unearthly slant \ look out, look out
\ it's right behind \ carrying a mound of
my hair strands \ sheeny shiny\ just-warm

hello, malaise

I like to look sexy in a grocery aisle, I
like to look like a black forest tartlet.
when standing at a window in my
underthings against the night opaque, I
conceive a person just beyond there,
clasping binoculars or bullets. I saw
the headline: *Woman Discovers Black
Widow Inside a Red Grape*, and now I
can't not dissect my produce into mush.
what I am feeling is not real, many would
say. the pharmacy finally spoke to me,
said: closed, please come back.

don't forget to send me courage

my online dress came already & I am
like this one good thank you. the
doctor said I could meet you at the
moment there in the orchard where
we stood sexual as cherries—stone
juice, red drupe. can you please send
me the address of the cold forest?
have you ever needed a phone call? I
am so sorry for leaving the house &
breadcrumb, catmint & delphinium.
where are we going to go in the big
world, in the big wound?

painbox

all nightfall brightly—a collision.

my brainache, my nape and temples

    bifurcated, poked through with a

    hairpiece, a circlet of rhododendron

I pry off entire. I never prayed in

my life—crest-fallen as a banshee.

    the nightfall spiteful, I was pressed,

    supine, tamped down to peat moss.

handful in handful, they went. and I

was stayed, laid under layers

    of pods, clay, already corroded.

Outburst as Darling

After *Darling* (2015)

I have one of those faces—bird-slender features, my starched and gothic collar,
hair dried in a flip or slipped into a tall bouffant. *Poor girl,* they said, *you're a doll,
a godsend*, they said. They forsake me in a lovely house with a bourbon decanter,
drop cloth shiver, gilded fiberglass, and beveled mirror. Soft lounge music and
fabric perfume pump. A banging metallic and hacksaw, an inverted cross against
my breastbone. Conjure me sinister, conjure the smog, the dress-maker scissors
un-making my gowns from the travel case. I won't be staying—my face rips and
I ripple inside this paint enamel, this satin wall.

Outburst as Samantha Hughes

After The House of the Devil (2009)

The night gets away from us. No moon visibility,
not after the stroke of midnight. I stroke the handset

    of the phone—my call cannot be completed as dialed,
    emergency. I'll be back in two shakes of a lamb's tail.

I wail in the boneyard, my nose-tip rose-cold,
my boiled wool mittens on a handgun. Is everything

    all right in there, in anywhere? In the frightmare,
    such unexplained events. I shoot against diastole,

you're saving me, incarnate devil, incarnadine
as cardinal birds, flocking over my ovaries.

Outburst as Sidney Prescott

After *Scream* (1996)

The echo is mine—the blood is wrong and it is also
mine. I use my set of lungs, thawed with splatter-movie.

Oh you dumb stud-bucket, you Billy-boy, shithead with
a blade. I'll draw blood from end to end, prick open your

scrotum, extract viscera. I stuff you with Jiffy Pop, your rind
supple like my White Adidas leather upper. My carpal bone

welted—give me a cold compress and let's boogie, the hoodie
trussed around my pubis. You say you have a *thing* for me—

so does everybody, every body where blood is found, throbbing
like a video cassette, a ribbon culled out of its casing.

notes to self

maybe I should stay up late & destroy myself/pop my polyester blouse diaphanous & spray ammonia on my computer & then it dies/in summer, I gasp in utter horror at my freckles/mistake them for unspecific bugs/ remember the mushrooms in the quadrangle are not trash/despite the sheen on them like stale bread loaves/& in my phone, there is my demon/ I clean him from the data cache/though he won't be disappeared for long/is it safe to eat a peach with bruise under/peach with visible cellular damage/I squash a hot spoon on this horsefly bite/in the sterling, I recognize myself like a magpie with a mirror test/I think I know why you threw me away

traumata

I crumple a little too much   come apart at the tomb entrance   your mausoleum
is my mausoleum   the eye crumbles   like a clementine, skinned   it's okay
it's okay it's okay you're okay   I behold the worst things   things near-dead
hemorrhage dribble   tremors   my cranium purrs   under a mink fur
an eiderdown duvet   it's okay it's okay   fitful, frightful animalcule
into the ground   a thicket of briars and halogen   my oxblood
nerve in shock   we belong in a modem   in a morgue
he and I   my demon with eyes   it's okay it's okay
it's okay   I'm okay   there is still starbright
phlox   silica glass   shellac nail   Prozac
it's okay to turn back, returning, to not
look elsewhere where there is no
blot, no blood clot, to daringly
be alone with a picture, to
leave it, no one harmed.

Notes

"aerial" is inspired by the fairy tale "Thumbelina" by Hans Christian Andersen.

"don't forget to send me courage" was created using predictive text software on a cellphone, inspired by the works of Laura Theobald.

"nuptial" is inspired by the fairy tale "Bluebeard" by Charles Perrault.

"Outburst as Becky Driscoll" is inspired by the film *Invasion of the Body Snatchers* (Don Siegel, 1956).

"Outburst as Carrie White" is inspired by the film *Carrie* (Brian De Palma, 1976).

"Outburst as Clarice Starling" is inspired by the film *The Silence of the Lambs* (Jonathan Demme, 1991).

"Outburst as Darling" is inspired by the film *Darling* (Mickey Keating, 2015).

"Outburst as Ginger Fitzgerald" is inspired by the film *Ginger Snaps* (John Fawcett, 2000).

"Outburst as Heather Donahue" is inspired by the film *The Blair Witch Project* (Daniel Myrick and Eduardo Sánchez, 1999).

"Outburst as Ivy Walker" is inspired by the film *The Village* (M. Night Shyamalan, 2004).

"Outburst as Jay Height" is inspired by the film *It Follows* (David Robert Mitchell, 2014).

"Outburst as Laurie Strode" is inspired by the film *Halloween* (John Carpenter, 1978).

"Outburst as Marcie Cunningham" is inspired by the film, *Friday the 13th* (Sean S. Cunningham, 1980).

"Outburst as Marion Crane" is inspired by the film *Psycho* (Alfred Hitchcock, 1960).

"Outburst as Mary Henry" is inspired by the film *Carnival of Souls* (Herk Harvey, 1962).

"Outburst as Melanie Daniels" is inspired by the film *The Birds* (Alfred Hitchcock, 1963).

"Outburst as Nancy Thompson" is inspired by the film *A Nightmare on Elm Street* (Wes Craven, 1984).

"Outburst as Nina Sayers" is inspired by the film *Black Swan* (Darren Aronofsky, 2010).

"Outburst as Rosemary Woodhouse" is inspired by the film *Rosemary's Baby* (Roman Polanski, 1968).

"Outburst as Samantha Hughes" is inspired by the film *The House of the Devil* (Ti West, 2009).

"Outburst as Sydney Prescott" is inspired by the film *Scream* (Wes Craven, 1996).

"Outburst as Thomasin" is inspired by the film *The VVitch* (Robert Eggers, 2015).

"painbox" was created with images generated from N+7 with Hans Christian Andersen's "The Little Mermaid."

The "traumata" series is concerned with images of body horror experienced through television, film, and the internet as it intersects with anxiety disorder and trauma.

Acknowledgments

I would like to thank the editors of the following journals, in which versions of these poems first appeared:

Always Crashing, "traumata" series
Black Warrior Review, "sensorium"
Cotton Xenomorph, "Outburst as Thomasin"
Dream Pop, "Outburst as Carrie White"
FIVE:2:ONE, "aerial"
Grist, "hello, malaise"
Horror Sleaze Trash, "Outburst as Jay Height"
Millennial Pink, "Outburst as Heather Donahue"
Miracle Monocle, "bauble"
New Delta Review, "Outburst as Sidney Prescott"
New South, "Outburst as Rosemary Woodhouse"
Ninth Letter, "Outburst as Laurie Strode"; "Outburst as Clarice Starling"
OCCULUM, "splint"
Passages North, "Outburst as Becky Driscoll"
Peach Mag, "dark webs"; "pain management"
Reservoir, "don't forget to send me courage"
Rogue Agent, "zoloft diary"
Spooky Girlfriend 7" Single, "ghazal with the city sparking"
TENDE RLOIN, "crepuscule"; "Outburst as Darling"; "Outburst as Ginger Fitzgerald"; "Outburst as Marcie Cunningham"; "Outburst as Marion Crane"; "Outburst as Melanie Daniels"; "Outburst as Nancy Thompson"; "Outburst as Nina Sayers"; "Outburst as Samantha Hughes"; "villanelle w/ anxious thoughts"
THRUSH, "notes to self"
Yemassee, "scab-picker"; "nuptial"
Yes, Poetry, "residence in a time of horror"

I would also like to thank the MFA program at Indiana University and my thesis committee, Adrian Matejka, Ross Gay, and Stacey Lynn-Brown, for their indispensable advice and support. This manuscript would not have come into being without you all. Thank you to Mary Biddinger and Amy Freels and everyone at the University of Akron Press. Thank you, family. Thank you, loved ones. Thank you, my love-person, Joe, and my fur-baby, Soup. Thank you, thank you, thank you.

Emily Corwin is a recent graduate of the MFA program
at Indiana University-Bloomington and the former Poetry
Editor for *Indiana Review*. Her writing has appeared in
Black Warrior Review, *Ninth Letter*, *New South*, *Yemassee*,
THRUSH, and elsewhere. She has two chapbooks, *My
Tall Handsome* (Brain Mill Press) and *darkling* (Platypus
Press), which were published in 2016. Her first book,
tenderling, was released in 2018 from Stalking Horse Press.
She lives and teaches in Michigan.

Printed in the United States
By Bookmasters